D0919145

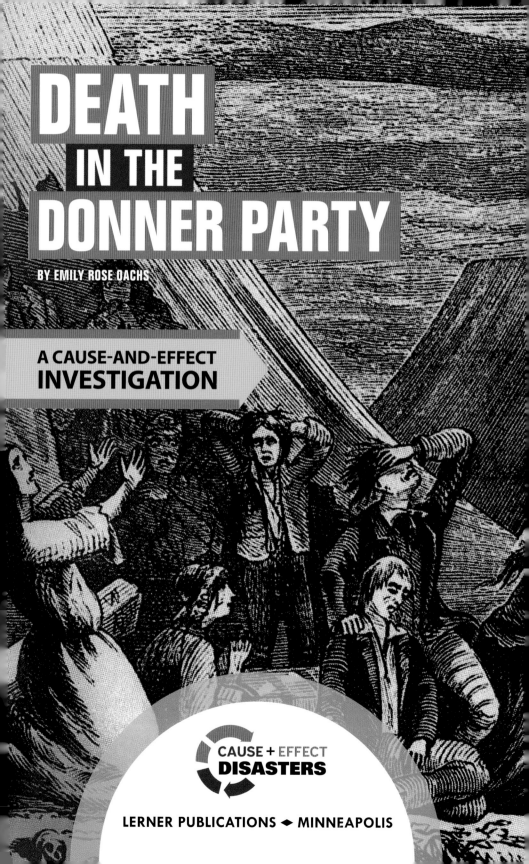

DEATH
IN THE
DONNER PARTY

BY EMILY ROSE OACHS

A CAUSE-AND-EFFECT
INVESTIGATION

CAUSE + EFFECT
DISASTERS

LERNER PUBLICATIONS ◆ MINNEAPOLIS

Lerner Publications Company
A division of Lerner Publishing Group, Inc.
241 First Avenue North
Minneapolis, MN 55401 USA

For reading levels and more information, look up this title at www.lernerbooks.com.

Content Consultant: Tim McNeese, Associate Professor of History, Department of History, York College, York, NE

Library of Congress Cataloging-in-Publication Data

Names: Oachs, Emily Rose, author.
Title: Death in the Donner party : a cause-and-effect investigation / by Emily Rose Oachs.
Description: Minneapolis : Lerner Publications, 2017. | Series: Cause-and-effect disasters | Includes
    bibliographical references and index. | Audience: Age 9-12. | Audience: Grade 4 to 6.
Identifiers: LCCN 2016008861 (print) | LCCN 2016009342 (ebook) | ISBN 9781512411157 (lb : alk.
    paper) | ISBN 9781512411263 (eb pdf)
Subjects: LCSH: Donner Party—Juvenile literature. | Pioneers—California—History—19th century—
    Juvenile literature. | Pioneers—West (U.S.)—History—19th century—Juvenile literature. |
    Overland journeys to the Pacific—Juvenile literature. | Frontier and pioneer life—West (U.S.)—
    Juvenile literature. | Sierra Nevada (Calif. and Nev.)—History—19th century—Juvenile literature.
Classification: LCC F868.N5 O16 2016 (print) | LCC F868.N5 (ebook) | DDC 978/.02—dc23

LC record available at http://lccn.loc.gov/2016008861

Manufactured in the United States of America
1 – VP – 7/15/16

TABLE OF CONTENTS

Chapter 1
A SHORTCUT WEST 4

Chapter 2
THE PASS CLOSES 14

Chapter 3
SNOWBOUND 20

Chapter 4
THE DONNER LEGACY 28

GLOSSARY 38

SOURCE NOTES 38

SELECTED BIBLIOGRAPHY 39

FURTHER INFORMATION 39

INDEX 40

A SHORTCUT WEST

Between 1840 and 1860, about 250,000 men, women, and children moved across North America. These emigrating pioneers abandoned crowded eastern states to settle territories in the West. They loaded their families and belongings into wagons. They set out on a journey that would take them about four months and cover more than 2,000 miles (3,200 kilometers). They crossed plains, mountains, rivers, and deserts. By 1860 these settlers filled the vast lands of Oregon and California.

Emigrating pioneers often traveled in covered wagons.

Sisters (*clockwise from top left*) Frances, Georgia Ann, Leanna, and Elitha were four of the five daughters of George Donner. They made the trek across country when they were ages four to thirteen.

In 1846 eighty-seven of those emigrants formed the Donner Party, named for its leader's last name. The families of Jacob Donner, George Donner, and James Reed formed the core of this wagon train. They had heard stories about the wonders California held. Similar to many other emigrants, they wanted to start new lives for themselves there. These three families were fairly wealthy. Emigrants who made the journey west needed to have money saved. The long journey meant a family would not earn any income for months. And, there would be more expenses when they arrived and set up their homes.

The three families were from Springfield, Illinois. In mid-April they set out for Independence, Missouri, with nine overflowing wagons pulled by oxen. They also brought cattle, including dairy

THE

EMIGRANTS' GUIDE,

TO

OREGON AND CALIFORNIA,

CONTAINING SCENES AND INCIDENTS OF A PARTY OF

OREGON EMIGRANTS;

A DESCRIPTION OF OREGON;

SCENES AND INCIDENTS OF A PARTY OF CALIFORNIA

EMIGRANTS;

AND

A DESCRIPTION OF CALIFORNIA;

WITH

THE DIFFERENT ROUTES

COUNTRIES;

AND

Hastings's guidebook described a shortcut to California.

cows for milk, to provide food on the trail and once they reached their destination. At Independence they joined forty-six other wagons heading to California, then a part of Mexico, in the Russell Party. This large wagon train started out on the Oregon Trail. They sometimes traveled 18 miles (29 km) in a single day. At night the camps were alive with music, dancing, and storytelling. But this good fortune would soon change.

Along the trail, the Russell Party met a messenger bearing an open letter for the pioneers. It was from the adventurer Lansford W. Hastings. The letter advertised a shortcut to California. It promised that Hastings would meet interested emigrants at Fort Bridger in modern-day Wyoming. From there, he would guide them along the shortcut.

The pioneers were already familiar with Hastings and his shortcut. Some were using his 1845 book, *The Emigrants' Guide to*

Oregon and California, as a guidebook on their journey west. Even Jacob Donner carried a copy in his packs. Hastings briefly described the shortcut in the book, even though he had never actually tried the route himself.

The trail west split at Little Sandy River. There, on July 20, Russell's company parted ways. Most families did not want to risk taking the shortcut. They continued on the northwestern route toward Fort Hall. But the Donners, Reeds, and a few other families turned southwest toward Fort Bridger. Soon, this small group elected George Donner as its leader. It officially became known as the Donner Party.

AGES OF THE DONNER PARTY EMIGRANTS

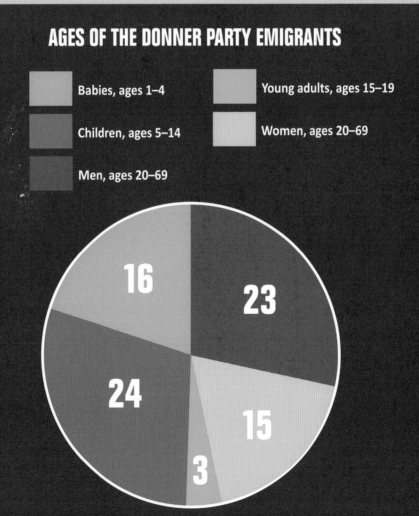

Babies, ages 1–4

Young adults, ages 15–19

Children, ages 5–14

Women, ages 20–69

Men, ages 20–69

16

23

24

15

3

Jim Bridger worked with Hastings and knew the West well.

On July 27, the Donner Party arrived at Fort Bridger. There, they learned more about the Hastings Cutoff shortcut. They heard it would shorten their journey by 350 to 400 miles (560 to 640 km). Jim Bridger, who worked with Hastings, promised the trail would be level and smooth. The pioneers would have to face only one waterless stretch of 40 miles (60 km), at most. Hastings, however, was no longer at the fort. He had traveled ahead with another wagon train. But he left word that any trailing wagons should follow his path.

The Donner Party still could have returned to the Fort Hall route. But the pioneers were lured by the promise of a shorter journey. So on July 31, the Donner Party started on the Hastings Cutoff. Sutter's Fort stood about 700 miles (1,100 km) away. The pioneers expected to cross that distance in seven weeks.

The first week on the cutoff went smoothly for the Donner Party. The pioneers traveled 10 to 12 miles (16 to 19 km) per day. But things changed near Weber Canyon. They discovered a note from Hastings in a bush beside the road. It claimed the trail through the canyon was nearly impossible to follow. Hastings said to send a messenger ahead to find him. He would then return to lead the travelers along a better route.

Three men rode ahead to find Hastings. But Hastings refused to return to lead the group. Instead, he joined one of the men on a mountaintop. From there, Hastings pointed out a course through the Wasatch Mountains. He had never tried this route before. But he thought it would be easier to travel than the path he had just taken.

The Donner Party followed Hastings's instructions. But they found what one member of the party later described as "uncharted wilderness." There was no trail at all. The emigrants had to clear their own road through the Wasatch. They cut down trees and underbrush. It took the emigrants six hard days to clear one 13-mile (21-km) stretch.

The pioneers emerged from the Wasatch on August 27. They were exhausted. Nearly a month had passed since they left Fort Bridger. But they had traveled only 36 miles (58 km) in twenty-one days.

Next, the Donner Party faced the Great Salt Lake Desert in present-day Utah. Hastings had claimed this desert was 40 miles (64 km) across. At its edge, they found a tattered note from Hastings partly attached to a board. It warned they would not find water for two days.

Desert still surrounded the Donner Party after two days. Their stores of water ran dry. Some people nearly died of thirst. The oxen that pulled their wagons also grew weak and thirsty. The pioneers unhitched the animals and drove them toward water. They planned to return later to retrieve their wagons. But some oxen ran away. Others dropped dead on the ground.

Again Hastings had misled the emigrants. It took them five days, not two, to cross the dry expanse. The desert was 80 miles (130 km) across. It was twice as wide as Hastings promised.

For one week the wagon train camped at the desert's edge. The pioneers needed rest after the challenging crossing. They also hoped to find their runaway cattle. While resting, the pioneers

The Great Salt Lake Desert is a dried-up lake. It gets less than 8 inches (20 cm) of rain each year.

saw their provisions were running low. They sent ahead Charles Stanton and William McCutchen. They would ride to Sutter's Fort and return with supplies for the wagon train.

The Donner Party started moving again in mid-September. Thirty-six cows and oxen had died or run away in the desert. The Reeds lost all of their cattle but two. They had to leave behind two of their three wagons. Two other families abandoned wagons. Many others left belongings, including furniture and books, at the side of the trail. The weary oxen could not handle the heavy loads.

When they left Fort Bridger, the Donner Party had hoped to be safely at Sutter's Fort in seven weeks. But more than seven hard weeks passed. On September 26, the Donner Party reached the Humboldt River. There the Hastings Cutoff met up with the California Trail. But hundreds of miles still separated the pioneers from California. Would they make it before winter snows blocked their path?

After traveling through the Great Salt Lake Desert, some of the oxen were too exhausted to continue on.

THE PASS CLOSES

The Donner Party had been told the Hastings Cutoff saved 350 to 400 miles (560 to 640 km). But it turned out to be 125 miles (200 km) longer. It cost the Donner Party about a month of travel time.

Hastings and his wagon train had already arrived in California. The other California-bound pioneers, including the Russell Party, arrived in early September. But the Donner Party lagged far behind.

The wagon train was struggling. Another desert crossing took its toll on the emigrants and their animals. The oxen had grown scrawny. Some had collapsed. Others were stolen and killed by American Indians.

To reach California, the Donner Party had to pass through the Sierra Nevada.

Food supplies, too, ran dangerously low. The pioneers cut their ration sizes. Some days they skipped meals. They were nearly starving. Still, the Donner Party pushed on into the Sierra Nevada.

The sharp, rugged peaks of the Sierra Nevada trail down the eastern edge of modern-day California. The Donner Party needed to cross Fremont's Pass and get out of the Sierras before winter snows blocked them into the mountains until spring. They were the last of the season's emigrants on the trail.

On October 19, Stanton met the party along the Truckee River, in the Sierras. McCutchen remained at Sutter's Fort, having fallen ill. Two Miwok Indian guides joined Stanton. The three men led seven mules. Meat and flour filled the animals' packs. The hungry emigrants rejoiced over the supplies.

Stanton also brought word about Fremont's Pass. Snow normally did not block the pass until mid-November, Stanton told them. This meant the Donner Party had a month to cross. With this news, the group decided to rest. They wanted to prepare for the hard upcoming journey. For six days they camped in the Truckee Meadows.

As seen in this 1865 illustration, migrants had to cross Fremont's Pass early in the season, before snow blocked the route.

From there, the pioneers continued toward the pass. Snowstorms had already blanketed the peaks with white snow. With each step, the drifts grew deeper. Waist-deep snow slowed the pioneers' progress to a crawl. Their oxen were starving and overworked. They struggled on the snowy route. Finally, they could no longer pull the heavy wagons. So the travelers abandoned their wagons. They slung their meager supplies across the backs of their bony cattle. Then they lifted their children into their arms and trudged up the mountain.

After a blizzard, tree branches weigh heavy with snow.

Eventually, snow buried the trail. The travelers could not continue. One night in late October, they stopped to camp within 3 miles (5 km) of Fremont's Pass. Stanton and one of the Miwok guides went ahead to find the route. They returned with word that snow had not yet blocked the pass. But the travelers would need to cross it before more snow fell.

The skies overhead looked threatening. Some pioneers wanted to continue before bad weather arrived. But they were exhausted. They could not travel any farther that day. They agreed to stop for the night and push ahead in the morning.

Dark clouds warned that more bad weather might be coming.

Someone lit a dead pine tree on fire in the makeshift camp. The pioneers gathered around its warm, leaping flames. Parents spread buffalo-hide blankets over the snow as beds for their children. Everyone bundled up warmly. They settled in for the night under more layers of blankets and cloaks.

That night the snow came. Fat snowflakes mixed with sleet. It fell hard and fast from the sky. The travelers could barely see. Mothers brushed piles of snow off their children throughout the night. In the morning, the world was unrecognizable. As one emigrant described it, "I found myself covered with freshly fallen snow. The camp, the cattle, my companions had all disappeared. All I could see was snow everywhere." One foot (0.3 meters) of snow had fallen in the night. Drifts 10 feet (3 m) high surrounded the travelers. What the emigrants most feared had happened. The pass was blocked.

Exhausted from traveling through the snow, the Donner Party made camp for the night.

SNOWBOUND 3

The pioneers started their Sierran winter already in tough shape. As one survivor later recalled, "We [were] . . . weary, already half-starved, and almost desperate." Now, with Fremont's Pass blocked by snow, they would have to wait until spring to travel again.

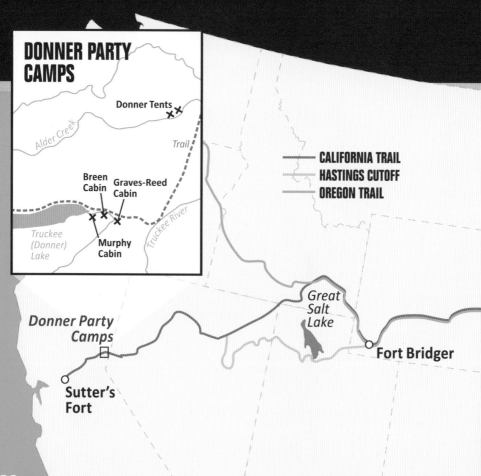

DONNER PARTY CAMPS

Donner Tents

Alder Creek

Trail

Breen Cabin   Graves-Reed Cabin

Truckee (Donner) Lake   Murphy Cabin

Truckee River

CALIFORNIA TRAIL
HASTINGS CUTOFF
OREGON TRAIL

Donner Party Camps

Great Salt Lake

Fort Bridger

Sutter's Fort

The Donner Party set up two separate winter camps. About sixty members of the party made camp at Truckee Lake. This lake sits at an elevation of 6,000 feet (1,800 m) in the Sierras. One cabin already stood beside the lake. The pioneers quickly built two more small log cabins nearby. The Breen, Graves, Reed, and Murphy families, along with some smaller families and individuals, stayed here.

The Donner families and a few of the other travelers made camp beside Alder Creek. They had lagged behind the other pioneers. The snow caught them as they camped about 6 miles (9.7 km) from Truckee Lake. About twenty travelers stayed there. They struggled to set up their winter camp. Snow interrupted their work building log cabins. So instead, they constructed crude tents using quilts, buffalo-hide blankets, and tree branches. These shelters offered little protection against the Sierran winter.

THE DONNER PARTY'S ROUTE

ILLINOIS

Springfield
○

Independence
○

MISSOURI

The Sierras are among the snowiest places in North America. Soon the Donner Party saw storms that raged for ten days. Heavy clouds dropped 4 feet (1.2 m) of snow in a single storm. Eventually, the snow lay as deep as 13 feet (4 m). So thick was the snow that Donner Party member Patrick Breen observed, "No living thing without wings can get about."

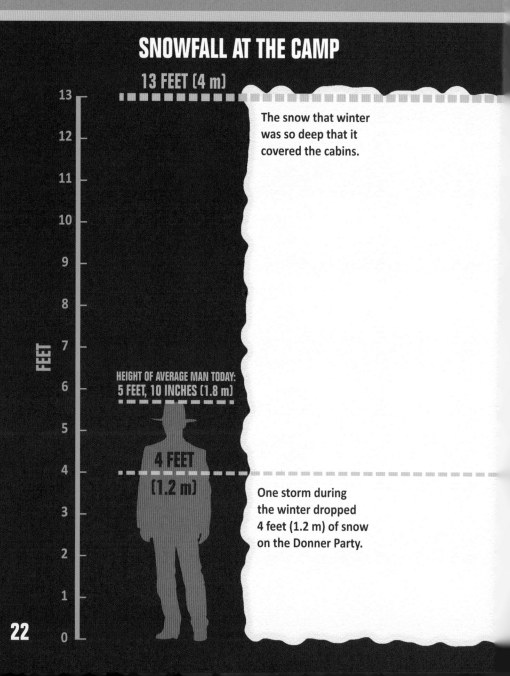

SNOWFALL AT THE CAMP

13 FEET (4 m)

The snow that winter was so deep that it covered the cabins.

HEIGHT OF AVERAGE MAN TODAY:
5 FEET, 10 INCHES (1.8 m)

4 FEET
(1.2 m)

One storm during the winter dropped 4 feet (1.2 m) of snow on the Donner Party.

FEET

13
12
11
10
9
8
7
6
5
4
3
2
1
0

This 1866 image of tree stumps cut by the Donner Party near Truckee Lake shows how deep the snow was at the time.

The deep snow made collecting firewood difficult. Men chopped down trees, but the trees then disappeared in the soft snow. The starving men struggled to haul the logs back to the cabins. During storms, nobody could leave the cabins to gather firewood. So sometimes they cut chunks of wood from their walls to fuel fires. Other times, the emigrants went without a fire. On these days, children stayed in bed to keep warm.

Provisions were scarce at the two winter camps. Stanton had brought much-needed supplies. But the Donner Party still did not have enough food for the winter. They had no bread or salt. And the travelers had lost more than one hundred oxen and cattle on their journey. Now the pioneers understood how important those animals could have been as they waited out the winter.

Some families were so hungry that they caught and ate field mice.

With their cattle, they likely would have had enough meat to survive until spring.

The emigrants' surviving cattle were thin and bony. But the pioneers needed as much meat as possible. So they butchered many of these animals. Then, during a storm, the livestock they did not kill wandered off. The deep snow made the animals impossible to find. The Donner Party had lost even more much-needed food.

The emigrants started to find food in unappealing places. They boiled bones for days to make a thin soup. After that, they burned the bones in the fire and then ate them. Families captured and cooked field mice. Some pioneers killed and ate their dogs. Even twigs and bark became meals.

Many pioneers used animal hides as cabin roofs. The hides blocked out the snow. But eventually the hungry families needed the hides for food. They boiled the hides, and the water became thick and sticky like glue. Then the pioneers swallowed the liquid.

The members of the Donner Party grew weaker each day. In December, the first of the stranded emigrants died. Five men died before Christmas. By January's end, fourteen people had perished.

On December 16, fifteen emigrants left the winter camp in an escape party. They became known as the "Forlorn Hope." Other parties had tried to reach safety. But deep snow and bad weather forced those groups to turn back. Only the Forlorn Hope escaped the mountains. They carried a small ration of food and wore homemade snowshoes. Of those fifteen, five women and two men survived. They arrived at an American settlement on January 17, 1847. The travelers had frostbitten and bloody feet. They were barely alive. But they sent help back to the other snowbound emigrants.

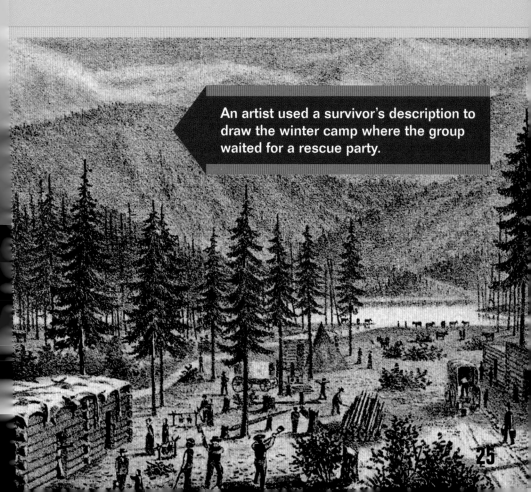

An artist used a survivor's description to draw the winter camp where the group waited for a rescue party.

On February 19, the first relief party arrived at Truckee Lake. There, the seven rescuers found the pioneers. They were just skin and bones and nearly dead. Some struggled to walk or stand. Snow completely covered the cabins. And the cabins were dark, dirty, stinky, and crawling with lice and mice.

For months the pioneers had seen only each other and snow. They could not believe that help had arrived. One woman asked the rescuers, "Are you men from California, or do you come from heaven?"

The rescuers handed out small portions of beef, flour, and biscuits. Then they gathered about twenty of the strongest emigrants. On February 22, the rescuers led this group out of the mountains.

Aid had come to the Donner Party, but nobody was safe yet. Even with the rescuers, the emigrants faced storms with no shelter and little food as they hiked out of the Sierras. Some pioneers died as rescuers guided them to safety.

The survivors were taken to Sutter's Fort.

Those left at the camp ran out of food. The provisions from the rescuers were not enough. Finally, the pioneers became desperate. They needed to eat or they would die. So some emigrants ate the bodies of the people who had already died. Cannibalism was the only way they could survive.

Three other relief parties came throughout the spring. They helped the pioneers who had been too weak to leave with the earlier parties. The rescuers led these survivors to Sutter's Fort. The last member of the Donner Party made it out of the mountains at the end of April.

Thirty-six of the party perished during the tragedy. One died early in the journey. Twenty-two died in the winter camps. Thirteen died as they tried to escape the mountains. Barely half of the party—forty-five emigrants—survived.

Patty Reed (right) was one of the children in the Donner Party who survived. She kept her doll (left) with her throughout the ordeal.

THE DONNER LEGACY

No single event stands out as the cause of the Donner Party disaster, but its effects have long outlasted the survivors. The natural landmarks of that snowy winter—Truckee Lake and Fremont's Pass—still remain. But their former names have been forgotten. The world now remembers them only as Donner Lake and Donner Pass.

A memorial near the site of the Donner Party's camp honors early pioneers who traveled west.

VIRILE TO RISK AND
FIND; KINDLY WITHAL
AND A READY HELP
FACING THE BRUNT
OF FATE; INDOMI
TABLE—UNAFRAID.

MAJOR DELAYS

August 6–11: 6 DAYS	The Donner Party camps at Weber Canyon for six days. Meanwhile, three men ride ahead to find Lansford Hastings for instructions.
August 12–27: 16 DAYS	The emigrants clear their own path through the Wasatch Mountains. It takes them fifteen days to travel 36 miles (58 km).
September 2: 1 DAY	At the edge of the Great Salt Lake Desert, the Donner Party camps for a day.
September 9–15: 7 DAYS	The Donner Party camps beside the Great Salt Lake Desert. They rest after the tough crossing and search for runaway cattle.
October 20–25: 6 DAYS	The Donner Party stops to prepare to cross Fremont's Pass.

Word of the Donner Party catastrophe traveled quickly. Over the winter, newspaper articles mentioned a wagon train trapped in the mountains. Coverage continued after the survivors were rescued in the spring. By midsummer, news of the disaster reached New York. Newspapers described the horrifying details of the Donner Party's winter.

A 2004 excavation in Truckee, California, revealed bone fragments from some of the Donner Party's first meals in the camp.

But this experience was not normal for emigrating pioneers. Few other wagon trains faced a fate like the Donner Party's. For over twenty years, large wagon trains crossed the United States. Some pioneers died from the journey's natural risks, such as illnesses and accidents. But most pioneers reached the West safely. Of all the emigrants who set out for California and Oregon, only 6 percent, at most, died along the trail. But the Donner Party lost almost half of its members. This was a result of the Donner Party's decision to put their faith in Lansford Hastings and take the Hastings Cutoff. The public came to fear the Hastings Cutoff. In time, the Hastings Cutoff was largely abandoned.

Most emigrants made it safely to their destination.

The number of pioneers moving to California dwindled in the following years. The Mexican-American War (1846–1848) in California was partly to blame. It is also possible that the tragic stories of the Donner Party convinced some families to turn toward Oregon rather than California. Migration resumed after gold was discovered near Sutter's Creek in 1848.

The California government sent aid to the travelers as the flow resumed. Late in 1849, many pioneers and their oxen suffered on the road. They had traveled across North America only to find little water and grass. Many pioneers had been ahead of them on the trail, and little food was left for livestock. The California government worried the emigrants would not cross the Sierras before winter. It gave $100,000 for the army in California to set up rescue and relief efforts. The money was used to pay people to meet the pioneers with water and fresh livestock along the trail. These helped the travelers arrive safely in California before winter. The government also did this in 1850 and 1852.

Newspapers and the public criticized the Donner Party. They thought it had dawdled on the road. They claimed the journey should have taken four and a half months, at most. The Donner Party could have avoided its fate if it had pushed harder. Newspapers also blamed the Donner Party's overloaded wagons.

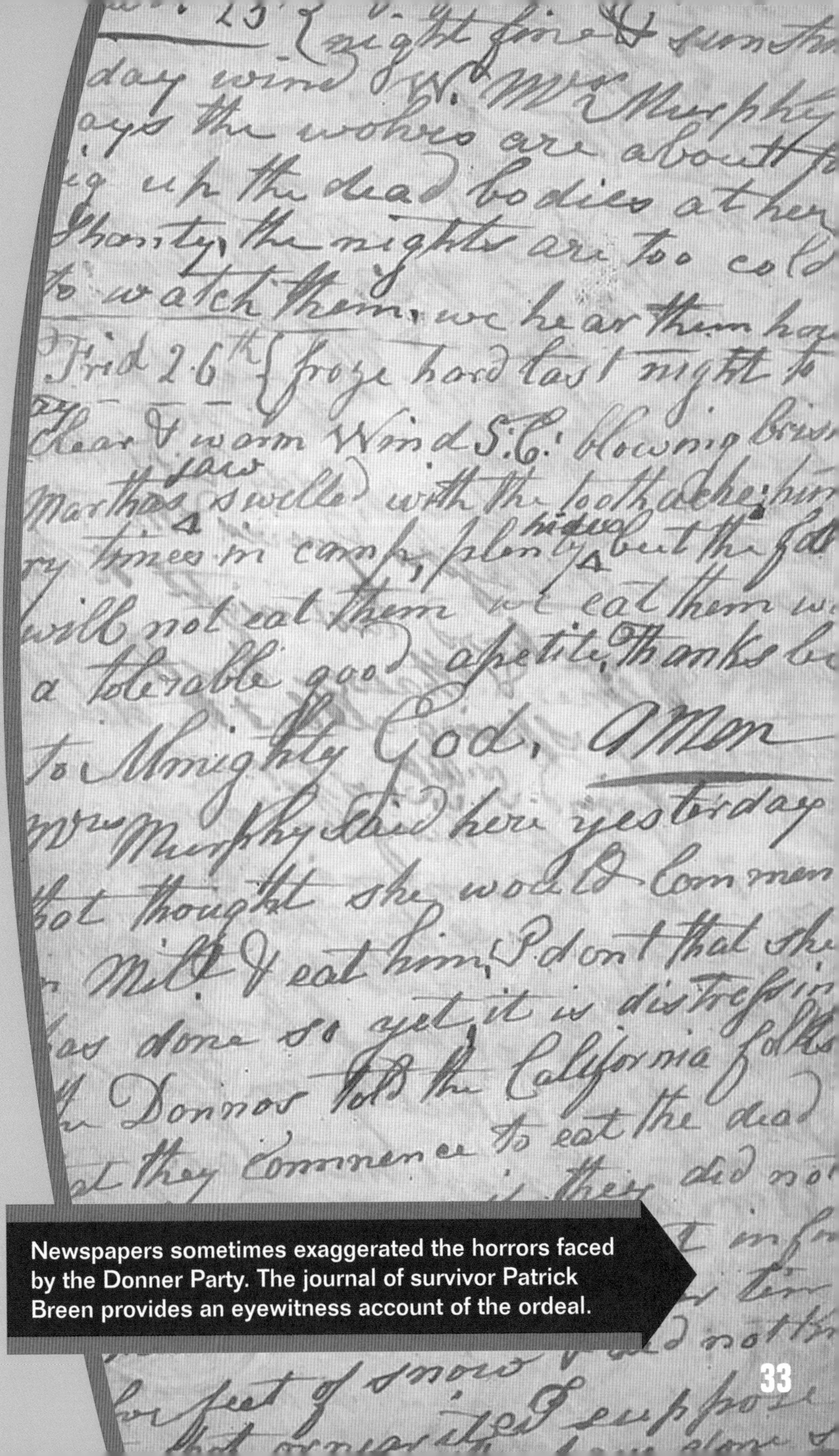
23 { night fine & sunshine
day wind W. Mrs Murphy
says the wolves are about to
dig up the dead bodies at her
shanty, the nights are too cold
to watch them, we hear them howl
Frid 26th { froze hard last night to
day Clear & warm Wind S.E. blowing briskly
Marthas jaw swelled with the toothache; hun
gry times in camp, plenty hides but the fol
will not eat them we eat them with
a tolerable good apetite. Thanks be
to Almighty God. Amen
Mrs Murphy said here yesterday
that thought she would commence
on Milt & eat him. I dont that she
has done so yet, it is distressing
The Donnos told the California folks
that they commence to eat the dead

Newspapers sometimes exaggerated the horrors faced by the Donner Party. The journal of survivor Patrick Breen provides an eyewitness account of the ordeal.

Emigration and Travel
Changed the Lives of Countless Ordinary People

The Sierra Nevada range forms a daunting barrier along California's eastern border. Majestic and imposing, these mountains have always tested anyone crossing from one side to the other.

Generations of Washoe used well-worn game trails to travel over the summit and throughout their homeland.

Hopeful emigrants followed with lumbering wagons, struggling towards an uncertain future.

Thousands of Chinese workers drilled and blasted tunnels through the mountains and laid track for the Central Pacific Railroad, which would connect California to the east.

Twentieth-century travelers took eagerly to new highways, motoring toward adventure.

Explore the many ways that the journey across these mountains changed the lives of people and altered the course of U.S. history.

California's Rugged Mountain Gateway

Lured by the promise of free land, many families looked west to start new lives. Between 1845 and 1848, about 2,500 people, among them the Donner Party, migrated to California. After months of travel, they encountered what 19th-century pioneer William Swain called "faces, long, back-breaking, leg-wearing mountains." Most found passage over these mountains through what became known as Donner Pass.

A Fateful Decision

Foot Rest

They claimed the heavy wagons slowed and exhausted the oxen. This created even more delays.

After the disaster, guidebooks warned against arriving at the Sierras late in the season. They encouraged pioneers to cross early to avoid the snows. One guidebook suggested that "to cross in safety [emigrants] must reach the [Fremont] Pass by the 1st of October," even though snow usually did not come until November.

Perhaps the greatest lesson learned from the disaster was best said by Virginia Reed, a member of the Donner Party. Reed was thirteen that winter in the Sierras. She described the ordeal in a letter shortly after she was rescued. In it, she advised, "Never take no cutoffs and hurry along as fast as you can."

CAUSE

The Donner Party decided to take the untested Hastings Cutoff route to save time.

Hastings Cutoff is longer and more difficult than the common trail.

Winter arrived early in the Sierra Nevada.

Beginning in February, rescue efforts took several months and started with the strongest survivors, leaving the others behind.

The story of the Donner Party was described in detail in newspapers around the country.

EFFECT

The journey took longer than expected and required the travelers to break their own trail.

The oxen and cattle were exhausted by the journey. Some cattle ran away. Others died on the trail. In total, the party lost more than one hundred oxen and cattle during the journey.

Fremont's Pass was blocked with snow. The Donner Party was forced to spend the winter in the mountains without enough food.

Those left at the camp quickly ran out of food. As the situation grew worse, some even ate the bodies of fellow travelers who had already died.

Hastings Cutoff was feared and largely abandoned. Some travelers may have chosen to head toward Oregon rather than California.

Glossary

cannibalism: the act of a human eating another human
emigrant: a person who moves away from his or her region or country
livestock: farm animals
meager: few, little
ordeal: a difficult experience
pass: a passage between mountain peaks
pioneer: a person who is one of the first to settle a new area
provisions: supplies set aside for later use
ration: the amount of food a person is allowed to eat at one time
wagon train: a group of wagons that carried settlers west

Source Notes

10 Virginia Reed Murphy, *Across the Plains in the Donner Party*, ed. Karen Zeihert (North Haven, CT: Linnert Books, 1996), 41.

19 C. F. McGlashan, *History of the Donner Party: A Tragedy of the Sierra* (Sacramento, CA: H. S. Crocker Co., 1907), 209.

20 Ethan Rarick, *Desperate Passage: The Donner Party's Perilous Journey West* (New York: Oxford University Press, 2008), 115.

22 Patrick Breen, *Diary of Patrick Breen, One of the Donner Party*, ed. Frederick J. Teggart (Berkeley, CA: The University Press, 1910), http://www.books-about-california.com/Pages/Academy_Pacific_Coast_History/Diary_of_Patrick_Breen_txt.html.

26 George R. Stewart, *Ordeal by Hunger: The Story of the Donner Party* (Lincoln: University of Nebraska Press, 1960), 152.

35 Dale Morgan, ed. *Overland in 1846: Diaries and Letters of the California–Oregon Trail* (Lincoln: University of Nebraska Press, 1963), 243.

35 George R. Stewart, *Ordeal by Hunger: The Story of the Donner Party* (Lincoln: University of Nebraska Press, 1960), 361.

Selected Bibliography

Breen, Patrick. *Diary of Patrick Breen, One of the Donner Party*. Edited by Frederick J. Teggart. Berkeley, CA: The University Press, 1910.

Burns, Ric. "The Donner Party." *American Experience*. Public Broadcasting Service, aired October 28, 1992. Transcript. http://www.pbs.org/wgbh/americanexperience/features/transcript/donner-transcript

Murphy, Virginia Reed. *Across the Plains in the Donner Party*. Edited by Karen Zeihert. North Haven, CT: Linnert Books, 1996.

Rarick, Ethan. *Desperate Passage: The Donner Party's Perilous Journey West*. New York: Oxford University Press, 2008.

Further Information

Books

Aronin, Miriam. *How Many People Traveled the Oregon Trail? And Other Questions about the Trail West*. Minneapolis, MN: Lerner Publications, 2012. Find answers to all your key questions about the Oregon Trail and emigrants moving west.

Hale, Nathan. *Nathan Hale's Hazardous Tales: Donner Dinner Party*. New York: Amulet Books, 2013. Read the story of the Donner Party in this graphic novel, which retells the disaster through the eyes of the Reed family.

Morley, Jacqueline. *You Wouldn't Want to Be an American Pioneer! A Wilderness You'd Rather Not Tame*. New York: Franklin Watts, 2013. Learn the hardships the average American pioneer faced on the journey west.

Websites

America 101: The Oregon Trail
http://www.oregontrail101.com
Check out this website for Oregon Trail information, fun facts, and historic sites, along with real-life diaries from the trail.

American Experience: The Donner Party
http://www.pbs.org/wgbh/americanexperience/films/donner
Take an in-depth look at the Donner Party's tragic fate and the factors that led to it.

Patrick Breen's Diary
http://www.books-about-california.com/Pages/Academy_Pacific_Coast_History/Diary_of_Patrick_Breen_txt.html
Read the text of Patrick Breen's diary, the only surviving diary written during the ordeal.

Index

Breen, Patrick, 22
Bridger, Jim, 9

cannibalism, 27

deaths, 25, 26, 27, 31
delays, 10–11, 13, 14–15, 19, 29, 35
Donner, George, 5, 7
Donner, Jacob, 5, 7

Emigrants' Guide to Oregon and California, The, 6–7

Forlorn Hope, 25
Fort Bridger, 6, 7, 9, 10, 13

Fort Hall route, 7, 9
Fremont's Pass, 15, 17, 20, 28, 35

Great Salt Lake Desert, 11, 29

Hastings Cutoff, 9, 13, 14, 31
Hastings, Lansford W., 6–7, 9–10, 11, 14, 29, 31
hunger, 15, 23–25, 26

McCutchen, William, 13, 15

oxen, 5, 11, 13, 14, 16, 23, 32, 35

Reed, James, 5
Reed, Virginia, 35
rescue party, 26–27
Russell Party, 6–7, 14

shelter, 21, 26
Sierra Nevada, 15, 21, 22, 26, 32, 35
Stanton, Charles, 11, 15, 17, 23
Sutter's Fort, 9, 13, 15, 27

Wasatch Mountains, 10, 29
winter camps, 21, 23, 25, 27

Photo Credits

The images in this book are used with the permission of: © Pictorial Press Ltd/ Alamy Stock Photo, p. 1; © Sasha Buzko/Shutterstock.com, p. 3; © Apic/Getty Images, p. 4; Eliza P. Donner Houghton/Internet Archive, pp. 5 (left), 5 (right), 25; © Wikimedia Commons, p. 6; Red Line Editorial, pp. 7, 20–21, 22 (chart), 29 (foreground); The Denver Public Library, Western History Collection, [Z-314], pp. 8–9; © m-kojo/iStock.com, pp. 10–11; © Bettmann/Corbis, pp. 12–13; © Zack Frank/Shutterstock, pp. 14–15; © North Wind Picture Archives, pp. 15, 18–19; © yanikap/Shutterstock.com, p. 16; © Rushtodanger/iStock.com, pp. 16–17; © Anna Rassadnikova/Shutterstock.com, p. 22 (man); Lawrence & Houseworth/ Library of Congress, p. 23 [LC-USZ62-27607]; © Victor Tyakht/Shutterstock.com, p. 24; Library of Congress, pp. 26–27 [LC-DIG-pga-03551]; © James L. Amos/ Corbis, p. 27; The Jon B. Lovelace Collection of California Photographs in Carol M. Highsmith's America Project/Library of Congress, p. 28 [LC-DIG-highsm- 23373]; © St. Nick/Shutterstock.com, p. 29 (background); © Debra Reid/AP Images, p. 30; © Everett Historical/Shutterstock.com, pp. 30–31, 32; © Bancroft Library/ University of California, Berkeley, p. 33; © Sam McManis/TNS/Newscom, pp. 34–35.

Front Cover: © St. Nick/Shutterstock.com, left; © North Wind Picture Archives, right.